POWER TO THE PEOPLE

ASCENDING BEYOND RACISM

Copyright © 2018

All rights reserved. Printed in the United States of America where Donald J. Trump is currently the 45th president.[1] No part of this book may be reproduced or transmitted in any form or by any means, electronic or mechanical, including photocopying, recording, or by any storage and retrieval system, without permission in writing from Hoston Enterprises, LLC and ZL Publishing House, except in the case of brief quotations embodied in critical articles and reviews.

Published by Hoston Enterprises, LLC and ZL Publishing House

Book Cover Design by Clinton J. Robinson Sr.
Book Cover Format by Emmanuel Gonzales
Interior Design by Christine Borgford, Type A Formatting

A CIP catalog record for this book is available from the Library of Congress.

Hoston, William T.
Power to the People/ by William T. Hoston Sr.

To contact the author, please visit: WilliamHoston.com

ISBN-13: 978-0-9992639-5-2 (paperback)
ISBN-13: 978-0-9992639-6-9 (ebook)

Made in the USA
10 9 8 7 6 5 4 3 2 1

POWER TO THE PEOPLE

ASCENDING BEYOND RACISM

William T. Hoston Sr.

PUBLISHING HOUSE

THANK GOD FOR TODAY!

WE ALL BLEED THE SAME COLOR.

TRUE LOVE SEES NO COLOR.

DEDICATIONS

To My Son
William Terrell Hoston Jr.
You were birthed to fulfill God's purpose for you
and take unconditional care of your mother.
You have the greatest mother in the world.
Daddy loves you.

Legend has it/ Aries are confident, determined, and courageous/ You will need these traits to lead the people/ William Jr., you are our shining Black and Brown prince/ Born to lead/ But you have to love the people/ To lead the people/

Lead by example/ For example, set an example, and make an example of/ This is the only way to win people's hearts/ For you are no Superhero/ You are a Normalman/ Whose powers are to give and love, and not seek in return/

I want you to know that wise men listen/ And then, *the wisest men follow their own direction*[2]/ Follow your heart, and it will lead to the answers/ For the most critical question is, 'how to love all human beings?'/

~Ode to W.T.H. Jr.

To My Brothers
Feddrick M. Hoston
Release Date: 01/20/2031
0000927443

Cleveland R. Wilborn
Release Date: 12/21/2019
0000807286

To My Uncles
Willie A. Holmes
Release Date: 05/14/2020
0000138511

Recardo J. Holmes
Release Date: Life in Prison
0000182963

Acts 3:19 reads, "Repent ye therefore, and be converted, that your sins may be blotted out, when the times of refreshing shall come from the presence of the Lord."

CONTENTS

ACKNOWLEDGMENTS	i
"TELL 'EM ABOUT THE 'DREAM,' WILLIAM JR., TELL 'EM ABOUT THE 'DREAM'!"	1
HEY YOU! GET OFF MY MOUNTAIN! HEY YOU! GET OFF MY CLOUD!	3
A STAR IN THE HEAVENS	4
DRAPETOMANIA, 1851	5
PREDICT THE BEHAVIOR OF THE OPPRESSOR	6
HOW COOL...PART I	10
HOW COOL...PART II	11
HOW COOL...PART III	12
HOW COOL...PART IV	13
HOW COOL...PART V	14
A NOTE TO BLACK FATHERS	16
EVENING STROLL, PART I	19
EVENING STROLL, PART II	21
EVENING STROLL, PART III	22
MEAN OLD WORLD	23

TOYS "R" US	24
LIFE IS TELLING ME…	25
HOW TO TREAT A SMASHED FINGER	30
I ONCE GOT LOST…	31
THE LIFE OF THE PARTY	35
UN-PRESIDENTIAL	36
TRUMPMERICA	37
MAKE CAMPUS GREAT AGAIN	44
I WISH, PART I	45
I WISH, PART II	48
I WISH, PART III	49
"TELL ME A BLACK JOKE."	50
LIFE IS A TRIP	54
WHITE SILENCE	55
MAN'S BEST FRIEND	56
#DEARBLACKATHLETE	60
A STERLING CASTILE	61
4-YEAR-OLD COMFORT	62
WHAT IT FEELS LIKE…	63
SHOOT AT WILL	64
FOR SALE	65

TARGET PRACTICE	66
MANN, TALK THAT TALK, PART I	71
MANN, TALK THAT TALK, PART II	72
MANN, TALK THAT TALK, PART III	74
BUG IN MY EAR, PART I	77
BUG IN MY EAR, PART II	78
BUG IN MY EAR, PART III	80
MISSING THE MARX	81
HOW DID WE GET HERE?	82
BLACK•ISH	83
I, TOO, AM FRUSTRATED	84
IMAGINE A BLACK CULTURE…	86
ABOUT THE AUTHOR	90
LIST OF PREVIOUS AND FORTHCOMING BOOKS	91

ACKNOWLEDGMENTS

All praise to my Lord and Savior, Jesus Christ. With Him, all things are possible. He has provided me with the four most influential women in my life, the late Mildred H. Hoston, the late Bertha-Mae Mitchell, Thelma C. Owens, and Janet Smith. I am a product of their hard work and sacrifice. In the words of Abraham Lincoln[3], "All that I am, or hope to be, I owe to my angel mother[s]."

To my beautiful and darling mother, Janet Smith, your examples of faith, courage, and sacrifice gave me much inspiration over the years to follow my dreams.

I want to thank my beautiful wife, Cecilia Hoston. I love you. You have given my life such love, happiness, and joy. My wife and my son, William T. Hoston Jr., are my world. I want to thank them for giving my life more balance and purpose. To my son, Daddy loves you. "You keep me smiling/ The things you do for me/ *I Wanna Thank You./*"[4]

A special thank you goes to June Marie Williamson Powell, the matriarch of 132 Villary Street, Belle Chasse, Louisiana. I appreciate you for loving me as one of your own children. We all miss you, Mama Junnie. Rest in paradise.

To the following families: Hoston, Zanders, Owens, Cosby, Mitchell, Duffey, Hooper, Nelson, Veus, Cooper, Franklin, Stewart, Gaines, Robinson, Gauthier, Anderson, Powell, Williams, Campbell, Thomas, Bolling, Hicks, Burrell, Green, Greenup, Hall, Isodore, Trufant, Laurant, Washington, Clements, Vance, Bonner, Sephus, Volley, Calice, Spivey, Wright, Long, Sanders, McQuarters, Baptiste, Davis, Barbre, Lee, Taylor, Carter, Garnett, Watson, Bennett, Swiner, Gabriel, Johnson, Rainey, Lain, Mauricio, and the whole, "132 Villary Street!" #229Americus. #504ForLife. #TheBestBank. #Hwy23ToTheEndOfTheEarth. #DTR.

To you whom I have not named, please know that even though you are not named in this book, I deeply appreciate what you have contributed to my life. Your contributions have helped this "Black boy fly."

Birth Place: Planet Earth
Race: Human Race
Politics: Freedom and Truth For All
Religion: Love For All
Resting Place: A Star in the Heavens
Legacy: William T. Hoston Jr.

WILLIAM T. HOSTON SR.

Psalm 119:28-31 reads, "28 My soul is weary with sorrow; strengthen me according to your word. 29 Keep me from deceitful ways; be gracious to me and teach me your law. 30 I have chosen the way of faithfulness; I have set my heart on your laws. 31 I hold fast to your statutes, LORD."

The enemy is a very good teacher. ~Dalai Lama XIV
...and I thank him, her, they, and them.

WILLIAM T. HOSTON SR.

The only thing more frightening than watching a Black man be honest in America, is being an honest Black man in America. ~Dave Chappelle

Racism is so American that when we are protesting racism, the average White American assumes we are protesting America. ~Unknown

WILLIAM T. HOSTON SR.

Them brothers [from New Orleans] said, "Don't go from written bars filled with rage/ To [academia] and your gilded cage/ Then forget it's people in the world still enslaved"/ I barbwired my wrist, and let it fill the page/ ~Black Thought[5]

For The Culture.
Period.

"ALL" HUMAN BEINGS ARE EQUAL!

BLACK
IS
BEAUTIFUL.

SAY IT LOUD, "I'M BLACK AND I'M PROUD!"

"TELL 'EM ABOUT THE 'DREAM,' WILLIAM JR., TELL 'EM ABOUT THE 'DREAM'!"

Adaptation of the 1963 *I Have a Dream* speech[6]

On April 4, 1968/ The world lost a King
On April 4, 2015/ A King was born

I say to you today, Black Americans [*applause*], we are living in trying times. My soul is weary. But we must be steadfast in our efforts to promote change. Many of us are mad at the world, and rightfully so. Please know that *in a mad world, only the mad are sane*.[7]

In the face of these trying times, I still have a dream. [*applause*] It is a dream deeply rooted in the social construction of race and the ideology of racism: It is a world without racism. I want to end racism! [*enthusiastic applause*]

I have a dream that one day White supremacy will be abolished: "We hold these truths to be self-evident, that all [human beings] are created equal." [*applause*] For White supremacy to end, White people must hold each other accountable. [*enthusiastic applause*] In the words of Socrates, "From the deepest desires often come the deadliest hate." [*applause*]

I have a dream that one day White law enforcement officers will be held responsible for their assault on Black bodies. [*enthusiastic applause*]

I have a dream that one day our nation will stop creating laws that further enslave Black women and men. [*applause*] We need to address the racially disparate treatment of Black Americans at every stage of the criminal justice system. [*enthusiastic applause*]

I have a dream that one day on the streets of Chicago, Baltimore, St. Louis, New Orleans, and cities around the USA, Black women and men will sit down together at the table of sisterhood and brotherhood and stop murdering each other. [*enthusiastic applause*]

I have a dream that my little boy, William T. Hoston II, will one day live in a nation where he will never, ever, be afraid to be Black. [*applause*] It is my dream that he will be able to "Predict the behavior of the oppressor," which will be a mighty weapon. [*enthusiastic applause*]

I have a dream that Black Americans will not have to show the USA that Black Lives Matter. [*enthusiastic applause*] Thomas Jefferson once said, "I tremble for my country when I reflect that God is just; that his justice cannot sleep forever."[8] These words hold truth. We will rise, and when we stand up, a new day will beckon. [*enthusiastic applause*]
Hoston, 2017

HEY YOU! GET OFF MY MOUNTAIN!
HEY YOU! GET OFF MY CLOUD!
(An Ode to The Dramatics)[9]

"The most powerful weapon on earth is the human soul on fire."
~Ferdinand Foch

Hey You! Get off my mountain!
Hey You! Get off my cloud!

There is a smile on my face creased from the hands of Harriet and Sojourner --- the strength of a Black woman. The truth is, Frederick pushed my smile upright, and Martin placed two Xs where the dimples needed to be to accentuate my confidence. It takes a village to build the confidence of a Black child, and a lifetime of rearing to bring up the rear.

Whatcha see is whatcha get. Black and beautiful. Black and bold. Black and confident. I am beautiful, bold, and confident, and more importantly, unapologetically Black. If the common denominator were removed, I would be "Free, White, and 21."[10] I would be a symbol of privilege, but I would not be the dramatic symbol of my ancestor's struggle.

Hey You! Get off my mountain!
Hey You! Get off my cloud!
Hoston, 2017

A STAR IN THE HEAVENS

From the grave/ There are a lot of Black folks who have passed to eternity/ Now living spiritually through me and others/ We will not fail them/ No way, no how/ Not in this lifetime/ Never!/

Future generations are depending on us to do what our ancestors called us to do/ The trickle-down effect of the generative power of Black solidarity/ History has shown us that destinies are at stake/

I, myself, am an accident of opportunity/ Generations removed as property/ I am the flesh of T'Chaka/ The offspring of Mansa Musa/ The child of Imhotep/ The son of Bell and Kunta/ A deity of life/ Born to help preserve the Black freedom struggle/ The slave who learned to read the Book of Exodus in the dark/ To bring truth to light/

When one world closes/ Another world opens/ Far, far away/ There is a life being formed/ Devoid of judgment/ Born free into the Heavens/ To one God/ Who protects human life at all cost/ He's got the whole world in His hands/

I am my ancestors' wildest dream/ Unapologetically *Black* and *Proud*/ A pillar of cloud by day and a pillar of fire by night/ Waiting for the eclipse of the sun/ To head toward Jerusalem/

I am *A Star in the Heavens*/ A diamond floating in the galaxy/ Who fell to the earth on 1619/ Into an enslaved world/ Now traversing the universal landscape/ Roaming like a swarm of Nats/ Pouring Black love out to Black people/ And my goal is to die empty/
Hoston, 2017

DRAPETOMANIA, 1851[11]

His-story has stood the test of time. Demigods are playing God because Michelangelo refused to present an Afro-Asiatic man to the masses. Images and idols ordain the White mind and elevate the White psyche --- *Whiteness as owners*. Whites as "holders" of Whiteness rule the world while Blacks as "slaves" of Blackness walk the earth in heavy standing. Two groups, *Whites* and *Blacks*, racialized in different ways --- One claiming ownership over the other --- forbidding freedom.

White supremacist ideologies lie under the thumbscrew of William Lynch (1712). White men in White coats with Black hearts stand around the Pick-a-Nigger table trying to diagnose the very people who they have enslaved --- *Blackness as property*. These White men are trying to diagnose why for God's sake would a people, who were once free, attempt to regain freedom.

A 50-dollar reward for any runaway slave in 2017.
Hoston, 2017

PREDICT THE BEHAVIOR OF THE OPPRESSOR

"Predict the behavior of the oppressor." The late Dr. William R. Jones, professor of African-American studies and religion, at Florida State University (FSU) used to always relay this message to his Black students. I met Dr. Jones in the Summer of 1997 prior to my first year in graduate school at FSU in a Black graduate student orientation program (BGSOP). He conducted a seminar session explaining his JAM and JOG oppression models. Each was an acronym: Jones Analytic Model (JAM) and Jones Oppression Grid (JOG). Dr. Jones supplied students with note excerpts from his unpublished manuscript, *Oppression-Centric Pedagogy 101: A Reference Manual and Workbook*, which details the models. These models were designed to navigate through the No Parity, No Prosperity (NPNP) minefield that sets institutional and systemic traps for Black folks to fail. He laid out the contextual and situational variables in each model to respond to oppression against Black folks at the micro and macro levels.

Many years later, I still remember two important phrases imparted by Dr. Jones (still written in my collection of notes from 1997): (1) "Predict the behavior of the oppressor," and (2) "If you do not understand oppression, you will be oppressed." He stressed that it was our responsibility, as Black Americans, to figure out the intent of the oppressor and decode the multiple facets of oppression. Dr. Jones noted that the symbol of the oppressor does not absolutely mean "the White man." He provided a simplistic definition of oppression, which is "The origin of difference; unjust treatment by anyone in a superior position." Any human being, regardless of race or ethnicity, can oppress another. In some cases, Blacks oppress other Blacks. However, as it relates to Whites, many have been given a surplus of institutional powers and privileges that allow them the ability to oppress other groups or subgroups.

In my 2014 book titled, *Black Masculinity in the Obama Era: Outliers of Society*, which provides an in-depth examination of the current state of Black males and identifies the impact of living in the Obama era, Black males chimed in on the life strategy of "predicting the behavior of the oppressor." Participants declared that it was imperative for Black males (and females) to have a heightened level of awareness and understanding of oppression when living, adjusting, and being situated in predominantly White environments. Floyd, Entrepreneur, 47, expressed, "White folks are playing a game that some Black folks still have not been able to figure out. Black males (and females) have to be strategic, educate ourselves, maximize our resources and assimilate without selling out. Our thinking needs to be two to three steps ahead when interacting with White folks. This is not condescending advice, but important advice for the success of Black people. Some of us are being oppressed every day and do not know it."

Participants believed that predicting the behavioral traits of Whites is necessary, and vital, for the continued plight of Black Americans. According to Sean, Manager, 27, "I don't trust White people. I'm the only Black manager at my job. It took me a while to understand that they will always do what is in their best interest. Each day when I get to work, I feel like I have to gauge the climate of the workplace. I have to be extra nice, more attentive, present my ideas in a non-threatening manner, and figure out who actually has my best interest." To affirm Sean's point, Black Americans must work to predict the behavior of the oppressor and not be oppressed. It is important for us to be able to decode the multiple facets of oppression. Lack of knowledge and awareness among Black Americans will continue the thriving nature of oppression.

In the book, the participants acknowledged that there is no accurate way to predict the behavior of the oppressor, however, understanding better the multiple facets of oppression reduces the ability for oppression to be used as a weapon against us. We need to gain a greater knowledge base of White supremacy, patriarchy, and economic,

societal, and cultural exploitation. In the end, it will benefit Black Americans in general, and also, help to foster spaces and societies that value all human beings.
Hoston, 2014

HOW COOL IS BLACK LIFE?

HOW COOL... PART I

How cool is it that the same God who created the Heavens and the Earth thought that civilization needed Black people throughout history to be enslaved, dehumanized, imprisoned, murdered, and recurrent victims of individual, systemic, and institutional genocide by the beneficiaries of White empowerment?

How cool is it?
Not cool at all.
Hoston, 2017

HOW COOL . . . PART II

How cool is it that the same God who created the Heavens and the Earth thought that He needed to invent a Devil to rival his existence --- the archenemy of God? And thus, the Devil was used as an antagonist to control the minds of slaves. Many slaves saw the spiritual Devil through a dual lens --- evil and moral. In the end, the spiritual Devil eventually manifested into a human Devil.

How cool is it?
Not cool at all.
Hoston, 2017

HOW COOL... PART III

How cool is it that the same God who created the Heavens and the Earth said through Biblical text that all good people would go to Heaven and all bad people would go to Hell? This is not an oxymoron. This is an open secret. Even Jesus went to Hell, but God resurrected Him. For Blacks framed as bad, is there an evangelical Heaven?

How cool is it?
Not cool at all.
Hoston, 2017

HOW COOL . . . PART IV
(Inspired by Uncle Tom's Cabin)[12]

How cool is it that the same God who created the Heavens and the Earth knew that it took some time to see that there is hope for the Pickaninny?

The Niglet can blossom into a "Good Nigger"
   With help from Eva's love

The World: How were you conceived?
Topsy: "I s'pect I just growed. Don't think nobody never made me."

It's hard, but we have to make it easier
   Topsy-Turvy

Oppression never taught Topsy how to love or feel love
   The weight of the world on frail shoulders

How could God allow such a crime upon humanity?

How cool is it?
Not cool at all.
Hoston, 2017

HOW COOL . . . PART V

How cool is it that the same God who created the Heavens and the Earth thought that He needed to shower the world with sorrow?

There is a cloud outside of my window
It holds the very thing that has rolled down my cheeks for the last 44 years: *Tears*

Rain mixed with tears makes a rainbow puddle
At the bottom of the puddle is joy
From the ribbon in the sky

Dancing in the rain is a beautiful art form, but crying in the rain is a beautiful form of stoic reckoning.

Rain mixed with tears makes a rainbow puddle
At the bottom of the puddle is joy
From the ribbon in the sky

To see myself dancing in the rain despite the tears that hold the embodiment of life rolling down my cheeks is when my heart became my home. The knock on the door is now familiar. On the other side is a rainbow puddle lying upon the front door that reflects the very thing that has rolled down my cheeks for the last 44 years: *Tears*

God placed the rainy days in my life to appreciate the brighter days.

How cool is that?
Very cool.
Hoston, 2017

I LOVE *MY* BLACK-BROWN SON.

A NOTE TO BLACK FATHERS
(Living Apart from Their Children)

Psalm 127:3-5 reads, "3 Behold, children are a heritage from the Lord, the fruit of the womb a reward. 4 Like arrows in the hand of a warrior are the children of one's youth. 5 Blessed is the man who fills his quiver with them! He shall not be put to shame when he speaks with his enemies in the gate."

Dear Black Fathers,

The intent of this letter is not to cast aspersions. There are a multitude of reasons for the number of Black fathers who do not get the opportunity to hug and kiss their young children (and older children) on a daily basis --- some good, some bad, some indifferent --- but nonetheless, there are reasons.

For generations, Black fathers have had to endure hollow statistics with no narrative to explain this structural and cultural problem. Despite the hollowness of these statistics, fatherlessness is a far worse perceived problem within the Black community than other communities.

This letter is not written to debunk the Black-fathers-being-absent myth, but rather, to ask Black fathers who do not see their young children (and older children) on a daily basis to *find* a way or *make* a way to see them. I know for some, "It's not that simple." Trust me, I know. But if you can, please *do* because you are missing out on some precious moments.

If you would please indulge me, let me tell you about some precious moments in my life. Since the birth of my son, William T. Hoston Jr., life has been filled with them. These moments have made me laugh tears of joy, cry tears of joy, and most importantly, made me reflect on the joys of life. He is the reason I live, but every day I die of suspense waiting and watching for all of the new things he does each new day.

Moments like, watching him emerge from the womb. It was nothing like the pretty picture shown on television. There was screaming. There was heavy breathing. There was blood. There was crowning. There was one last big push. And then there was a miracle.

Moments like, looking into his face after he was born. He is I, and I am him. Whatever he is, I am. He is a reflection of me. We are one.

Moments like, watching as he took his first steps at 10-months-old. With all his might, he walked toward me and fell into my arms. Fathers are supposed to defy gravity.

Moments like, hearing his cries early in the morning for me to come and get him out of his crib. "Daddy, come get me!" While I lie in bed hoping that I am dreaming, his cries grow louder. "Daddy, come get me!!!" When I enter his room and try to explain to him the importance of being a big boy and sleeping in his crib, his reply is, "I don't want to be a big boy right now, I want to get in the bed with momma and daddy."

Moments like, getting him dressed for daycare. "Let's get dressed for daycare," I tell him while he watches *Color Crew* on the television. "I don't want to go to daycare. I want to go to work with daddy," he replies. At two-years-old, he has mastered the art of being cunning. "Daddy, I love you. I want to be chillin' like a villain all day with you." LOL. He makes me happy for no reason.

Moments like, dropping him off at daycare and he gives me the itinerary for his pickup. "When you pick me up, we are going to go and get ice cream. And see the doggies and fishys (at Petco). And go to Chuck E. Cheese. And go home and take a bath. And watch Peppa Pig on the iPad. And you read to me. And then I go to sleep in my crib like a big boy."

Moments like, picking him up from daycare. There is no greater joy than picking him up from daycare and when he sees me, he yells, "My daddy is here! Bye-bye. See you tomorrow. Let's go daddy!" The full-out-sprint daddy hugs never get old. The surprising thing is, he still remembers the itinerary. "Ok, let's go and get ice cream now."

Moments like, the other day, when I took him with me to Hobby Lobby. Recently, his grandfather began to give him money. He now knows that money can buy things. When he asks me for money, I jokingly ask him, "Can I fart on your head first?" and he will say, "Yes." In Hobby Lobby, he wanted money to buy candy in the checkout line. When I told him that he did not have any money to buy candy, he asked could I "fart on his head" for a dollar. When I told him, "No," he screamed at the top of his lungs and put his head in my butt, "Please daddy, fart on my head." Needless to say, we walked out of the store after that embarrassing, but funny moment, with a bag of skittles.

Moments like, putting him to bed every single night. When he is asleep in my arms, I examine him from head to toe. He looks just like me. Then I think about his mannerisms. He talks like me, and walks like me. Then I think about the quirks we share. We both like ketchup on our eggs. We both like to eat BBQ sauce by itself. The thing I think about the most is how much I love him, and how much he has meant to my life. I could not imagine not seeing him every single day --- waking up to him, and falling asleep to him. It would hurt me too much. He falls asleep in my arms and from my arms goes into his crib. When he says, "Good night, Daddy," it solidifies that I had a "Good day."

Black fathers, I too, have personally experienced life without a father. Therefore, this letter comes from a genuine place. It comes from a place of love.

In conclusion, I will say that if there is no way, *find* a way or *make* a way. Precious moments are happening every single day that you are not able to see and be a part of.

Hoston, 2017

EVENING STROLL, PART I

On the evening stroll, my son and I beat up the hardwood floors and door panel getting the tricycle out of the front door. The threshold is too narrow to exit, but we find a way to maneuver it shifting from one side to the next.

"We did it, Daddy!"

Juice ☑
Snacks ☑
Music ☑

"The wheels on the bus go round and round..."

He is in his own world. The one where the wheels on the bus never stop. His feet are peddling, but Daddy is performing the labor of love --- pushing him to the rightful destination --- maneuvering the tricycle at an enjoyable pace to absorb the brevity of human life. The sun dances off of my shoulders while shadowing his presence. This is our moment to be whole.

All he wants to do is enjoy his multi-color goldfish crackers.
"Red one, Daddy."
"Green one, Daddy."
"Yellow one, Daddy."

The lines are blurred by him calling me Daddy and us listening to, "Daddy finger, Daddy finger, where are you?"

"I'm right here, son," thinking to myself. Enjoying this lovely day. Enjoying this lovely stroll. Enjoying our time spent together.

It is in this absorption of the moment that I soak in the glory of our lives before he has to meet the world. The memories that reside within this father and son moment are the ones that God wants us both to cherish.
Hoston, 2017

EVENING STROLL, PART II

My son was speaking to me while peddling his tricycle and eating multi-color goldfish crackers.

He suddenly sees a lizard lurking in the bushes: "Don't you bite me, lizard! I'm a tell my Daddy on you!"

Him now speaking to me: "Get'em Daddy!" He fortifies that my job is to protect him.

My son will be a lonely God
   the bottom of life is crowded
   the top of life is awaiting his presence
   humility will keep him in the balance

Knowing that my presence is visible
   will afford him to be the quiet mind
   in the midst of chaos

He will live a full life in his own world
   so he won't have to die in another world

Humbled in birth
   he will be ordained in death

My son: "Don't you bite me, lizard! I'm a tell my Daddy on you!"

Life is funny
   thus, I'm grinning from ear to ear

Do I scare away this lizard and defuse my son's fear
   allowing me to be the hero at the moment
   or just tell him "Daddy will protect you?"
Hoston, 2017

EVENING STROLL, PART III

My son: "What's Daddy's teacher's name?"
Me: "Daddy is the teacher."

My son: "Daddy, teach me then."
Me: "Son, I've been teaching you since you were born."

I will teach you that love is a beautiful emotion
   It overlooks imperfections and hides flaws

I will teach you that love will never forsake you
   It will only cast aside the things that do not have purpose

I will teach you that love sees no color
   It will, in spite of this, try to define you

I will teach you that love does not shoot at podiums nor balconies
   It will, however, assassinate Black prejudice and White racism

I will teach you that love traverses the universe
   It brings the greatest joy
Hoston, 2017

MEAN OLD WORLD
(Sam Cooke version)[13]

This is a mean old world to try and live in all by yourself…

When my wife had my son/ The ugly truth/ Turned into a beautiful lie/ No more fibs about lonely happiness/ Only the truth about my joy and pain/

Walking into the house in the evenings/ I strip myself of the "isms," "phobias," and "gers" placed throughout the day/ I shed the embattled armor of hate/ Then my son coats me with love/ And my wife hardens the layers/ To prepare me for tomorrow/ Where I venture back into a world where I serve/ Despite the fact, some people think I am merely a servant/

I take all of the "Daddy, I Love You's"/ And place them into the four chambers/ Then the next day/ I shoot from the heart/ Targeting hate/ To make this world a better place for him/
Hoston, 2017

TOYS "R" US

No, it didn't matter
   that he had a Schwarze Sonne on his neck at the time

It's two days before Christmas
   and we are both in Toys "R" Us trying to get all things
   that represents the movie, *Cars 3*
   both of our sons love Lightning McQueen

He told me his son loves the *Cars* franchise
   my son loves *Cars* too

No one knows what the future holds
   friends or foes
   but for the moment
   our kids have similar interests
   not influenced by hate
Hoston, 2017

LIFE IS TELLING ME...

Lately, I've been having
  a reoccurring dream
    about an unknown elderly, Black woman
    named Brenda

She is sitting on the river bank
  with a fishing pole in her hand
    baiting the hook with a worm
    while singing *Hard Times* by Ray Charles[14]

Out of this dream
  is a Freudian-like condensation

Brenda teaches me how to rig-a-line
  while listening to my life story

She is talking to me
  about life and fatherhood
  and I am listening to her
  about life and motherhood

She keeps humming the song
  "Talkin' 'bout hard times, hard times
  Who knows better than I?"

Brenda teaches me how to catch and release
  while conversing about alleviating emotional pain

Brenda teaches me how to catch the biggest fish of my life
  while telling me to change my mindset

WILLIAM T. HOSTON SR.

This dream
   all, which equals, one dream symbols
   makes me question whether Brenda is my long-lost mother
Hoston, 2017

AMERI*KKK*A THE BEAUTIFUL.

WE BUILT THIS JOINT.

STILL NIG.

HOW TO TREAT A SMASHED FINGER

On December 14, 2007, I graduated with my Ph.D. I had officially entered "a" Caucasian door. On the way in, while pointing in appreciation to the abolitionist who had granted me access, one of the three fingers pointing back at me got smashed in the unlocked door. It was an incredibly painful experience. I proceeded to the restroom to soak my finger in cold water to reduce the swelling. There was a lot to ponder in this moment.

When I returned to the door rather than closing it shut, I left it ajar to allow caution to the wind. Then I placed an emergency key under the mat in case of permanent closure for more to enter.
Hoston, 2010

I ONCE GOT LOST…

I once got lost
  in the maze of acceptance

What my life stood for
  became secondary
  for the falsehoods of White validation and Black approval

Attempting to exercise Whiteness
  in a Black shell
  is impossible

Attempting to exercise Blackness
  in a Black shell
  is impossible

When I realized there was no way
  to escape from White validation and Black approval
  in this sweet land of liberty
  my life projected onwards and upwards
Hoston, 2017

MY RAGE WILL *NOT* FIT ON THIS PAGE.

LOVE TRUMPS HATE.

MAKE AMERI*KKK*A LOVE AGAIN.

THE LIFE OF THE PARTY
(Inspired by Gil Scott-Heron)[15]

Republicans have done a great job of drawing an imaginary line of race to divide poor White and poor Black people. Led by Trump, the Grand Old Party (GOP) has normalized racism and racial controversies to fit their political agenda. Republicans and conservatives have turned their backs on the rest of America. Of the 535 in Congress, who will stand for the people when the revolution comes?!? Who will craft a "Bill of Love" to Trump hate?!? **There is too much *party & bulls**t* in Congress.**

When the revolution comes, where will the congressional Democrats be? The revolution will not be televised on C-Span. Behind closed doors, votes will be cast to better White America. The Democratic party—or at least, part of it—will be trying to fight on behalf of racial and ethnic minorities. For the conservative Democrats, talks to help racial and ethnic minorities will soon turn to talks to maintain the status quo. Our American citizenship and long-form birth certificates will not matter. All Americans are not born alike. **There is too much *party & bulls**t* in Congress.**

The revolution will not be televised. We all know this. Thus, what even matters anymore? *Nothing.* Hope is all but lost in a unified government where lies are designed to evoke racial resentment and create more nationalist soldiers who direct their hate toward racial and ethnic minorities. **There is too much *party & bulls**t* in Congress.**

#BlackNBrownFuturesMatter
Hoston, 2018

UN-PRESIDENTIAL

Unstable genius. Unqualified. Incompetent. White mediocrity. Thin-skinned. Small-minded. Divisive. Racist. Sexist. Misogynist. Xenophobic. Narcissist. Sociopath. Delusional. Soon-To-Be-Ex-President. Whom will move to a "shithole" to escape reality.
Hoston, 2018

TRUMPMERICA[16]

I have a great relationship with the Blacks. I've always had a great relationship with the Blacks. -Donald J. Trump

The 2016 presidential election cycle brought out the worst in the American people. "We The People" displayed our divisions even more than we had done in 2008 and 2012 when the first Black president, Barack H. Obama, was on the ballot. In the quest to vote for the lesser of the two evils, "We The People" showed just how evil "We" can be toward one another.

During this presidential election cycle, "We" emotionally invested in a dangerous form of democracy. "We" voted for Democratic nominee Hillary D. Clinton because some of the American people despised now President Donald J. Trump's comments about women, Hispanics, Muslims, immigrants, and Black Americans. "We" voted for Trump because some of the American people believed Clinton could not be trusted after the Benghazi attacks, FBI email probe, her neo-liberal stances, and the patriarchal culture of the United States of America (USA). When the final tallies were calculated, Trump was declared the victor. Clinton had won the popular count by nearly three million votes, Trump had won the Electoral College vote (306 - 232), and a sizeable portion of the American people had not participated in the electoral process. Despite our feelings toward the two presidential candidates, our job as American citizens was (and continues to be) to safeguard American democracy and maintain collective harmony to move this country forward and avoid a new American Civil War. Instead of accomplishing this goal, the impetus behind the cast of our votes further propelled the notion that "We The People" are not, in fact, the "United" States of America.

The election of Trump as the 45th President of the USA is seen in the eyes of many American citizens as the greater of the two evils. During the presidential election cycle, he tore the scab off of the wounds of discrimination, racism, misogyny, sexism, and xenophobia, and then showed how the idea of capitalism and restoring hope for most White Americans after the Obama presidency can speed the healing for a certain faction of the country while ostracizing the remaining populace. In the aftershock of his victory, Trump's election to office has presented a devastating blow to women's rights, LGBTQIA rights and protections, disrespected the wishes of the Rock Sioux tribe, created a Muslim ban, and vowed to build a wall to keep undocumented Mexicans in their home country. Much of this extreme ideological push is due to his ability to sell fear and impart coded racist language while on the presidential campaign trail.

Trump made wealthy White men, college-educated White women, White working-class Americans, older White Americans, and White college non-graduates as a fragmented collective believe that equality for others equals oppression for them. In reality, the Trump Administration has continued a societal and cultural way of normalization where "We The People [of Color]" are forced to accept deep-rooted conservatism as the ideological structure in this country and conform to their practice of using executive orders to frame the USA in the way they see fit. His short time in office has been viewed as the restoration of Whiteness (and White identity) in the post-Obama presidency.

In the first 100 days of Trump's presidential reign, he had signed 32 executive orders and 29 bills into law.[17] He had signed more executive orders than any president since Harry Truman and more bills than the previous five presidents in office. His most hasty political and legislative actions targeted Hispanics, Muslims and immigrants, made citizens devoid of health care, and cut substantial funding to vital programs. The rest of his actions were glorified press releases and rollbacks of legislation from the Obama Administration.

An *ABC News/Washington Post* poll showed that his approval rating dove to a new historical low of 42 percent and not just among Democrats.[18] Former President Gerald Ford has the second lowest approval rating, 48 percent, at the 100-day mark. It seemed clear that the very people who voted for Trump now regretted their decision.

However, in spite of his low approval numbers, 96 percent of Trump voters said they would support him again.[19] Fifty-three percent of his base called him a "strong leader."[20]

In the best of all possible worlds, White voters who regretfully supported Trump would admit they made a mistake and align with liberal Democrats, racial and ethnic minorities, women, LGBTQIA people, and the few Republicans who voted against Trump to resist his presidency. President Trump, himself, admitted that "[Being the President of the United States of America] is more work than my previous life. I thought it would be easier."[21] Despite his formal admission of not understanding the precise requirements of the office, many of his supporters view economic, social, and political progress as a zero-sum game, and as a result, the election and presence of Trump is advantageous to their societal positioning. But many have yet to realize that Trump fooled them. Their attitudes and behaviors are reminiscent of President Lyndon B. Johnson once saying, "If you can convince the lowest White man he's better than the best colored man, he won't notice you're picking his pocket." Despite this, with Trump in the Oval office, there remains the ability to maintain the social construction of Whiteness as the ranking hierarchy of race. This ideology works within the parameters of their normative privilege to allow them to gain a better quality of life.

What does this mean to the Black community? Alternatively, in the words of President Trump, what does this mean to "the Blacks"?[22] There exists a large population of Black Americans who believe that Obama's symbolic presence and actual presidential influence did not align to have a more substantial effect on Black America as a whole and the continuation of Black advancement. To this end, as we enter the Trump presidential era, what will it mean for the Black experience in the USA?[23] President Trump knows Obama could have done more specifically to address Black interests, and he is eager to reverse Obama's few race-related legislative accomplishments by any means necessary.

Trump made an empty plea on the campaign trail to Black Americans while speaking to a majority White crowd in Michigan. He conveyed a direct message to Black Americans by stating, "You're living in poverty, your schools are no good, you have no jobs, 58% of your youth is unemployed -- what the hell do you have to lose?"[24] In a similar speech to Black voters, Trump contended:

> Look, it is a disaster the way African-Americans are living, in many cases, and, in many cases the way Hispanics are living, and I say it with such a deep-felt feeling: What do you have to lose? I will straighten it out. I'll bring jobs back. We'll bring spirit back. We'll get rid of the crime. You'll be able to walk down the street without getting shot. Right now, you walk down the street, you get shot. Look at the statistics. We'll straighten it out. If you keep voting for the same failed politicians, you will keep getting the same results. They don't care about you. They just like you once every four years — get your vote and then they say: 'Bye, bye!'[25]

The implications of this post-slavery rhetoric carry a consequential burden for the Black community. President Trump has been strategic in his messages to the Black community with the following understanding: First, his election to the Oval office comes after twice electing the nation's first Black president. According to political analyst, Van Jones, Trump's election was the result of a "White-lash" against a Black president.[26] President Trump campaigned directly to those who harbored feelings of White racial resentment like David Duke from Louisiana who is an American White nationalist and former Imperial Wizard of the Ku Klux Klan (KKK). On the day of the 2017 presidential inauguration, Duke tweeted, "We did it! Congratulation Donald J. Trump President of the United States of America!"[27] The KKK as a group and the Alt-Right, a group with an extreme far-right wing ideology that contains White supremacists, Neo-Nazis, Odinists, and more, support Trump as well.[28]

President Trump is vastly aware that he has the eyes and ears of the most radical White men to be the embodiment of his political message.

He refused to disavow the support of these individuals during his campaign and has regularly retweeted their messages all while once proclaiming to be "the least racist person that you have ever met."[29] Moreover, after Trump was sworn in as president, *The Daily Storm*, an American neo-Nazi website, speculated that he would remove White nationalist groups from the Countering Violent Extremism (CVE) list. They wrote on their website, "Yes, this is real…Donald Trump is setting us free."[30]

Second, during the Obama Administration there needed to be the origin of a Black Lives Matter (BLM) movement to address the deaths of unarmed Black men by some White law enforcement officers. This decentralized movement was sparked by national protests against a criminal justice system that allowed these officers to deal with Black men overaggressively. In most cases, unarmed Black men were fatally shot, and the officers involved were neither indicted by a grand jury nor convicted of such crimes. This lack of accountability has created a culture of civil unrest and distrust among members of the Black community who sought to challenge the inbuilt institutional and systemic racism and discrimination entrenched in the system.

President Trump's rhetoric has indirectly posited a question for conservatives to challenge the legitimacy of Obama's presidency by asking: *Why would a BLM movement need to be created under the administration of the first Black president?* He knows that some Black Americans are disappointed that Obama did not adequately address this concern. Obama was thrust to publicly discuss these racial controversies after civil unrest from the BLM movement and the Black community.

Third, President Trump's election offers up as proof that Black bodies moving through White spaces in American society will be met with White resistance. The rhetoric and actions of reducing Black Americans to "the Blacks," warning BLM members not to be "violent disrupter[s]" on the White House government website on his first day in office, and empowering Attorney General Jeff Sessions to undo the criminal justice policies under the Obama Administration that targeted Black Americans, shows that he will not wholly embrace the significance of preserving Black human life.[31] After President Trump empowered him, Sessions then gave a directive to federal prosecutors to seek maximum punishment for drug offenses. This directive by Sessions will eventually lead to the "War on Drugs 2.0," which will send more Black Americans to prison.

Patrisse Cullors, one of the founding members of the BLM movement, said at the 100-day mark, "45 has proven to be one of the most dangerous human beings on the planet; we must resist his regime and build a movement in the millions."[32] The framework of White empowerment that President Trump is attempting to solidify further is being met with some resistance from liberals, racial and ethnic minorities, women activists, LGBTQIA activists, and some Republicans. But make no mistake, a real, radical left movement is needed to offset the early momentum of the Trump Administration.

In the words of President Trump, "What the hell do you have to lose?"[33] The answer from Black Americans is: "Everything!" This question is symbolic of the beginning of the erasure of the Black identity under his administration. He ran on the slogan, "Make America Great Again," which is considered a strong euphemistic phrase closely aligned to a period in American history where White men made laws that disproportionally affected Black Americans. From the first 100 days in office, it appears that how the Trump Administration will interpret the meanings of race and ethnicity will be conditioned by a shifting societal and cultural context that reestablishes White empowerment in the post-Obama presidency. The Trump Administration is built around the ideological makeup of White supremacists. He has placed people in key positions such as Steve Bannon, the former White House "chief strategist" and mastermind behind many of the early executive orders, who in the past openly advocated for White nationalism, and ran the Breitbart website that created a platform for the Alt-Right.

For these reasons, Black Americans must not simply correlate the election of President Trump as just the reinvention of a White president to occupy a traditional place in American history. Trump is dangerous, very dangerous to the human survival and well-being of Black Americans.

In the words of the legendary writer, James Baldwin, "To be Black and conscious in America is to be in a constant state of rage." Thus, for the next four years (and possibly eight years), the Black experience in White America will continue to be a daily out-of-body feeling of demoralization. To combat this, Black Americans must be resilient and work against the institutional and systemic powers that continue the societal and cultural war against us.

MAKE CAMPUS GREAT AGAIN

The choice is clear/ Some want to make campus great again/ "Unite the Right"/ Free *White* speech/ From students to staff to faculty to administrators/ This is a fragmented neoplantation/ Headed by hooded Ph.D.s/ Who teach the very people Trump marginalizes/

They are unmoved/ Standing on the table for justice/ However, sitting down for activism/ Conservative fascists/ In an Ivory tower/ Confirming that you are only as sick as your secrets/

Unorthodox communication/ The blasphemers walk in privilege/ And talk down upon the masses/ They live upon the false love of public approval/ Unbeknownst to them/ It is detrimental to their psyche/ 40% of the time they walk around living a fantastic lie/ The other 60% they attempt to justify insanity/ Hoping that time does not take advantage of them/ Playing the Trump card for the anti-intellectualism in American life/

This is a Turning Point USA on American campuses/ The path to righteousness is led by "very fine people" wearing tan khakis and white polos and carrying tiki torches/ Shouting "Blood and Soil"/ On American soil/ For the right to lead an American conservative movement/
Hoston, 2017

I WISH, PART I

This is hyperbole, or is it...
My words will be taken out of context, or will they not...
What is a Black professor in America allowed to say?
Luckily, my feelings are not subject to peer-review.

I wish I could be a White male professor for a day at a Predominantly White Institution (PWI). Life would be great. In stark contrast, the Black professor's burden carries weight.

I do not want just to be *any* White male professor; I want to be *that* White male professor. The one who fully understands his White male privilege and takes full advantage of it. I would not exercise my privilege to harm others by being a self-centered, pompous, egotistical maniac. I would only exercise my privilege to advance my own career. Surely, the two personas of privilege are mutually exclusive.

I wish I could get up in the morning, wash my face, brush my teeth, put on my clothes, eat breakfast, kiss my wife and son goodbye, and say to myself, "I am headed to a workplace that will allow my potential as a professor to fully flourish." To the contrary, I say each morning, "God, please shield me from the weapons that will form due to my confident Black male demeanor."

I wish I could walk into the building, bright-eyed and bushy-tail and greet each person in my path with great warmth knowing that preconceived stereotypes will not be my identification. To the contrary, racial stereotypes of Black professors are formed every day --- from White administrators, White faculty, and White students --- who believe that our mere existence is a microcosm of affirmative Black action.

I wish I could be a part of the Monday morning banter about their weekends --- family trips, children gatherings, etc. --- followed by me overhearing them talk in the hallway, "My wife had a really good time with your wife this weekend," said John Doe to Tom Doe. To the contrary, John Doe says to the others as I walk toward the crowd of White male professors, "Shhh, William is coming." Their body language and voice tone changes. Upon seeing me, John Doe asks aloud, "How was your weekend, William!?"

I wish I could be privileged to White male conversations that do not include women and racial and ethnic minorities. For example, John Doe tells Tom Doe, "Make me the chair of your promotion and tenure committee. I'll make sure you receive excellence marks." Or, "You got this. No worries." Unfortunately, this is the definition of 'social promotion'. These are the systemic and institutional conversations that define White male privilege in the academy.[34] To the contrary, I can outperform White male professors and still be made to feel like my work is less credible --- "presumption of incompetence." My race and gender-specific publications will be viewed as inferior.[35]

I wish I could walk into a classroom and teach to a class full of White students without feeling like I have to be damn near perfect each and every class period.[36] There is always that one young, White male student who thinks he knows more than me and will challenge me at every turn. I will never forget my first semester as a teaching assistant in 1997 at Florida State University (FSU), one of them wrote on my teaching evaluations, "He teaches very good for a Nigger." In 2008 at Wichita State University (WSU), one of them wrote, "I like him, but he wants the Nigger [Obama] to win." To the contrary, what is even sadder is that a number of them will give me low teaching evaluations because their identities and experiences have never included the undying support of a Black male who wants to see them maximize their potential in life.

I wish I could mentor students of all races and genders without judgment. To the contrary, a rumor here, a rumor there, rumors are everywhere. A fabrication here, a fabrication there, all of which, makes up the fabric of White supremacy. Fabricated claims that indict Black professors, but are tore to shreds to exonerate White professors. They will sully your name, defame your character, and then claim "absolute White privilege" in the court of public opinion. At the end of the day, there will be no apology.

I wish I could be near the end of the workday, ready to pack my things, and be excited about returning to work the following day hoping that it will be different. It will not. In short, it will be more of the same --- lack of institutional support and change, the absence of true diversity, and academic blackballing toward those who do not support an outdated paradigm, which all results in a toxic environment for most Black professors at a PWI. Nonetheless, I will return. I will return the next day not as a privileged White male professor, but as a frustrated, exhausted, wishing for the best, Black male professor, hoping that my efforts in creating change will one day help an upcoming, young Black professor.
Hoston, 2017

I WISH, PART II

This is hyperbole, or is it…
My words will be taken out of context, or will they not…
What is a Black professor in America allowed to say?
Luckily, my feelings are not subject to peer-review.

That awkward moment when a White student who said they "really enjoyed" your class and how you are "the best professor they've ever had" go out of their way to avoid you in public when they are with their White parents.

#ItsOkToBeWhite/ It's Ok to enjoy the class of your Black, Brown, or Yellow professor/ #ItsOk Hannah, Maddie, and Claire/ #ItsOk Lucas, Connor, and Hunter/ #ItsOk for White students to learn in the presence of forced assimilation/ For the mind is a canvas/ And it needs color from all walks of life to bring it to life/

This is hyperbole, or is it…
My words will be taken out of context, or will they not…
What is a Black professor in America allowed to say?
Luckily, my feelings are not subject to peer-review.

That awkward moment when a White student who said they "really enjoyed" your class and how you are "the best professor they've ever had" introduces you to their White parents in public and refers to you as "Mr. Houston" instead of "Dr. Hoston." Then proceeds to tell their parents "This is one of the professors at the school." And their parents say to you, "Nice to meet you, Mr. Houston. How long have you been adjuncting?"
Hoston, 2017

I WISH, PART III

This is hyperbole, or is it...
My words will be taken out of context, or will they not...
What is a Black professor in America allowed to say?
Luckily, my feelings are not subject to peer-review.

'Twas a wish of thee
  to wake up in a world of academic freedom

I wish I could live in a state of non-consciousness
   a paradoxical experience
   but consciousness drives the mind
   and it feeds the righteous soul

The most conscious people are often the most melancholy people
   therefore, allow me to cry for a lifetime in this profession
   in a state of rage

This is hyperbole, or is it...
My words will be taken out of context, or will they not...
What is a Black professor in America allowed to say?
Luckily, my feelings are not subject to peer-review.
Hoston, 2017

"TELL ME A BLACK JOKE."

What do you call a Black man who earns a Ph.D.?
"Good Nigger."

The Ph.D. did not liberate me/ As I was miseducated it would/ The shackles on my hands and feet extended to my mind/ The old me and new me remained/ A distinction without a difference/

At the Ph.D. graduation/ I said to my Massa professor/ "Chains ain't right for Niggers, Doctor E!"[37]/ He hooded me anyway/ Gave me my *Certificate of Freedom* from the U.niversity of N.egro O.ppression (UNO)/ And then led me to the Underground Railroad/

It was there/ Harriet was waiting for me/ With a gun in one hand and a slave Bible in the other/ On the ground was a bag full of disguises to integrate/

Harriet said to me, "Choose the proper disguise. But never shuck and jive for the masses."/ "Yes, Moses," I replied./ "Don't become an emasculated Black man seeking validation in an academic culture that sells achievement to the highest bidder/ And does not affirm the actions of the achiever/ Excellence will not be rewarded/ Yet, subservience will/ What weapon will you choose to outthink the oppressor? Choose wisely."/ "Yes, Moses," I replied./
Hoston, 2014, 2017

NO MORE RACISM.

KKK.

ALT-RIGHT- DELETE.

LIFE IS A TRIP

Some days I genuinely get a kick out of life...

A racist-old-White man who I once came in contact with
  put his foot out to trip me

Years later, I saw the man with his Black-White-mixed granddaughter

I fell to the floor to justify his previous action
Hoston, 2017

WHITE SILENCE

At the criss-cross
   of a Black life, we find
   the truth is that White silence causes commotion

Bang! Pow! Boom!

White accountability is, without question, the criss-cross
   to promote change
   however, White silence guarantees privilege
   a privilege not afforded to Black madness

Those who remain silent are responsible[38]

Question: If Black women are so angry and Black men are so dangerous, where are all of the Black nationalist hate groups destroying America?

Answer from White America: White Silence
Hoston, 2017

MAN'S BEST FRIEND[39]

There is an old Dachshund that barks
   very loud throughout the day

The SJWs have offered
   to put him out of his misery

He is barking at muh oppression
   showing his teeth
   and his dog collar reads, "14/88"

The dog is trying to defend his race
   in dog years, he was born on January 1, 1863
   in human years, he died on November 4, 2008
   and then rose from the dead on November 8, 2016

His bark is worse than his bite
   woof = Nigger
   woof = Kike
   woof = Spic
   woof = Hajji
   woof = Bitch

One day, at the crack of dawn, the dog broke from his chain
   and was found playing with a group of young Black children
   the dog could see disappointment in his owner's eyes

The next day, the owner decided to put the dog down
   the owner realized he could no longer train his best friend to hate
Hoston, 2017

BLACK LIVES MATTER.

WHERE WAS "ALL LIVES MATTER" FROM 1619 TO 1965?

DENIAL OF RACISM IS RACISM.

#DEARBLACKATHLETE

William C. Rhoden laid the blueprint.....But he put it in a book..... Fuckkkkkkkkkkk.....The Black athlete does not read.....They run, throw, catch, tackle, dribble, and dunk.....And then let Massa beat them for sport.....In sports.....A physical escape from the realities of slave life...This is the double entendre of the Black athlete.

When Kap knelt.....The Black athlete resisted.....When Trump spoke.....The Black athlete knelt.....Generations of SOBs called by name who do not know their rights, but know their place.....They responded to Massa in a knee-jerk reaction.....A chain reaction of mental slavery.

The Black athlete who speaks out against racism and discrimination..... Makes White America uncomfortable.....Their words attack the conservative narrative that uses the successful Black athlete to argue that race no longer matters in this country.

Know Your Rights[40].....Because a modern-day protest has emerged..... And divided the ungrateful Black athletes who will not "Shut up and play football" from the Forty Million Dollar Slaves.[41]
Hoston, 2017

A STERLING CASTILE

**Another day. Another hashtag. Another trending topic.
  A legal lynching. #AltonSterling #PhilandoCastile**

On the day after/ A Black Queen has to wake up without her Black King/ Black families suffer the same Black tragedy/ In a Black home where he lifted the Black curse/ The historical voodoo still looms over their Black souls/ Left to be comforted by an innocent child, "It's OK, I'm right here with you, momma."/

You have to be awake to know/ But they want us to defend ourselves against what cannot be foreseen/

You have to be alive to live/ But they ultimately decide our fate/

You have to care to value/ But they don't care/

**Another day. Another hashtag. Another trending topic.
  A legal lynching. #AltonSterling #PhilandoCastile**

An imaginary schema safeguards Whiteness to live in Utopia/ It is difficult to police the White imagination/ It fears gold-plated teeth and a "wide set nose"/ Meanwhile relegates Blackness to a place of eternal brutality/ Our tragic experiences are only an illusion/

Blacks are dying in a non-fictional war/ Against individuals/ Who make false assertions to describe reality/ Only to become fictional Heroes/ After they pull the trigger/ Captain Americas/ Who wear Black badges of honor/

In the end/ Black Americans are living in a deadly imbalance/ Hoping that today is not *the* final day/
Hoston, 2016

4-YEAR-OLD COMFORT

"Mom, please stop cussing and screaming 'cause I don't want you to get shooted,'" said the 4-year-old daughter in an attempt to comfort her mother, Diamond.[42] They both sat in the back of a police car. The mother in shock because she has just seen her boyfriend, Philando, murdered. The 4-year-old in a state of calm tells her mother, "I can keep you safe."

This is a reversal of caregiving roles. There is an unbearable sadness in the moment. The truth is, there is no truth. The problem is not the problem. The problem is, the false truth among those who make laws to benefit the powerful further and ignore laws that further oppress the powerless.

Only a lie will return this situation to normalcy by saying, "It's OK. I got it, OK." But everything is not OK. A routine traffic stop turned into a murder scene --- Black PTSD. After 29 hours of deliberation over five days, there is another jury acquittal of a law enforcement officer --- White IDGAF.

White Americans dictate the pace of justice. Therefore, they cross the tape before we do and hold the 'participation trophy' in great honor. There is no honor in that. It only sends a dangerous message to the masses. We are not all winners.

The sound of innocence speaks to all of us.

"I wish this town was safer," cried the 4-year-old.
Hoston, 2016

WHAT IT FEELS LIKE …

The jury is in/ The Boys in Blue/ Have been found innocent, again/ Goddamn!/ I can't even leave the courtroom/ Because we hitched our wagon to the criminal justice system/ And the emotional weight of the verdict/ Won't let us move/

My Aunt Mabel is crying/ My Uncle Avon is holding back tears/ An exercise in White supremacy/ A moment made for silence/ Quite the reverse, the loud sound of crying makes me think/ Think thoughts/ Loud thoughts/ Very loud thoughts/ My cousin, Wee-Bay, gives me *that* look/ But we don't see eye-to-eye/ Lex Talionis/ He is willing to take an "L"/ And wants me to walk the "Long" road with him/ Shittttttttttt/ My mind is racing/ I'm pacing back and forth/ Trying to get Brother Mouzone on *The Wire*/ I have a proposition for The God/

Finally, my uncle sees me pacing back and forth/ He's the one who taught me the chokehold that changed Jody's life/ It's hard to see him live for the rest of his days without his baby boy/ My uncle: "Don't do it, Neph. You're the noble one. We need you to make peace. The game ain't in you. There's games beyond the games. Don't worry though, Omar comin'."/ When he said it, I got it, but didn't understand it/ He wanted Jesus to be a fence/ But the Boys in Blue hopped over it/ And stole one of our family's most prized possessions due to mistaken identity: **Our young Black king/**

Dear White readers: This is the raw emotion of a broken family. This is what it feels like to the family, friends, and community when a White law enforcement officer fatally shoots an unarmed Black male and the criminal justice system fails them.

No Justice, No Peace
Hoston, 2014

SHOOT AT WILL

Shoot at Will. In a figurative sense, but not a literal sense. However, those who have a concealed carry and fear for their lives believe that death is without exaggeration.

Shoot at Will. In an analogous space, shooting Will is like shooting Trayvon --- two Black American male metaphors --- one alive, one dead, but both could occupy the same space and time at any given time. Trayvon's death broke the figurative threshold of exhaustion. Literally, he is no longer with us. Figuratively and literally, Black Lives Do Not Matter.

Shoot at Will. Consequently, in a literal sense, I walk gently on the earth awaiting.
Hoston, 2015

FOR SALE

Ernest Hemingway once wrote a six-word short story - It read, "For sale: baby shoes, never used."

William T. Hoston Sr. once wrote a six-word short story - It read, "For sale: Black bodies, barely used."
Hoston, 2017

TARGET PRACTICE[43]

After slavery and into the early 1900s, a game called "Hit the Nigger Baby" was popular for entertaining White families in the South. The purpose of the game was to use a ball to target and hit the bodies of living and breathing Black babies.[44] There was still a source of elation in the brutality of young Black bodies, even after the brutal whippings, lynchings, and killings during slavery when physical and deadly violence against Blacks was normal and legitimate.

More than a century later, White Americans are still playing racial games that target and project the imagery of killing Black people, in particular, Black males. News stories are emerging where White gun show vendors, owners of gun ranges, and police officers are using racist posters and mugshots of Black males for target practice. For instance, in 2015, one gun show vendor in South Dakota was selling racist targets that displayed a grotesque caricature of a Black male. At the top, it read, "Runnin' Nigger Target." When asked by a local news reporter why the targets were being sold, the vendor replied, "Why aren't they? They're just targets."[45] In a more disturbing story, sniper team members of the North Miami Beach police department were caught using mugshots of actual Black males for practice. This story became known when Army National Guard Sergeant, Valerie Deant, who was with her Guard unit at the facility for weapons qualification, saw a bullet-riddled target sheet that contained a picture of her brother, Woody Deant.[46]

North Miami Beach Police Chief, J. Scott Dennis, who admitted his officers "could have used better judgment," was in many ways dismissive of the magnitude of their actions.[47] He denied his officers engaged in racial profiling, but stressed that the targets were "vital for facial recognition drills."[48] Chief Dennis told news reporters, "There is no discipline forthcoming from the individuals regarding this…We utilize an array of pictures…We have an array for Black males. We have an array for White and Hispanic males."[49] In a later interview,

Chief Dennis said facial recognition drills were important to police training "so the sniper can practice exactly picking out the right target and avoid killing the wrong person in a real-life situation."[50]

The deeper correlation of these racist law enforcement practices and real-life situations gives rise to questions regarding the priming of White police officers to see Black males as sub-humans who are targets, typical offenders, and symbolic assailants. During a period in American society, when the relationship between White police officers and unarmed Black males is already strained, why would officers continue to engage in haphazard, irresponsible practices that further exhibit a deeper, systemic problem?

The answer: *They don't care about us.*
Hoston, 2015

TOO BLACK, TOO STRONG.

WE WILL *NOT* BE SILENT.

BLACK LIBERATION AIN'T FREE.

MANNN, TALK THAT TALK, PART I

In 2016/ The voices of the silent majority were no longer silent/ They spoke loud and clear/ Giving "Us" eight years/ From January 20, 2009 to January 20, 2017/ To believe that "We" mattered/ White guilt/ And then they used the ballot like a bullet/ A 187 to the post-racial myth/ The revenge of the White voter/ A modern day White-lash/ The reckoning of the post-truth/

Mannn, Talk That Talk

They used an American Firearm Icon/ To shoot through the bullet-proof vest of democracy/ And then used Susan B. Anthony's great-great-great granddaughter to cast the fatal vote/ She told the polls one thing/ And then got on the patriarchal pole for Donny/ Pimpin' ain't no illusion/ Where dem dollas at?/ Hold on, Bill is at the bar getting $1's/ Remember, strippers are humans, too/

Mannn, Talk That Talk

Farewell to the CEO of USA, Incorporated/ "Change We Can Believe In" was all a 'Game of Charades'/ I'll give you four years/ To act out this word: "F-E-A-R."/ Barry's election and presence woke the monster/ Victor Frankenstein's creation is now the POTUS/
Hoston, 2016

MANNN, TALK THAT TALK, PART II

Written on the 100th day of the Trump Presidency

Where in the hell is the Magical Negro in government?/ Pardon my French/ Je suis désolé/ But I need the Black man who was once the face of an American Empire/ To help to destroy it/ Let me rephrase, I need the Black man who was against populism, but wanted to be popular/ To denounce the popularity of his apprentice/ Let me say it another way, I need the Black man who once told me, "Yes, We Can."/ To finally tell me, "No, We Didn't."/ So I can come to grips with this mass hysteria/

Mannn, Talk That Talk

Let me be polite and diplomatic, I need the Black man who is considered by some to be "One of the greatest presidents in American history."[51]/ To prove his worth/ Elusive optimism is not a sign of failure/ But perpetual neoliberalism can tarnish a legacy/ And hurt human life/ I can't make political sense of it all/ Democracy must have died in the darkness/ She is no more/ From drone strikes to the Mother of All Bombs/ She has become a bully/ And threatened to kill the messenger/

Mannn, Talk That Talk

CRTL-*ALT-RIGHT*-DELETE/ MFen-kksjxjbsnnhdjfhsnndnfbfjdbd-Ass-jsbxhhdjsbdJhusbdbjsbdlalxjhhjsndhhdjdhqpsjxbxhdhejdjks hd-Holes/ This is me typing in a passionate rage/ Pounding the keyboard/ Writing a love letter to White supremacy/ Words of affirmation/ Searching for the right hashtags on Twitter/ To join the conversation at 3 a.m. in Deep-Red America/ The Internet is a Blackhole/ An *ALT-RIGHT* landmine/ To disable those who fight for equality/ This is bigger than the D's vs. R's/ This is about the crazies who stir the pot of wisdom/ With alternative facts/ To feed the masses goulash/

Mannn, Talk That Talk

America, the Beautiful/ Oh, you can be so ugly without makeup/ Your foundation has made reward rare/ And punishment common/ In a land where *my* Black forefathers died/ We are all stories/ Bound by loose-leaf paper/ Some narrated by White revisionists/ Others narrated by the discretionary powers of America/ The rest narrated by lost truths/ To construct the best tale/

The Black story is a short story/ When the pen writes in Red blood/
Hoston, 2017

MANNN, TALK THAT TALK, PART III

I got a letter from the government/ The other day/ I opened and read it/ It said: "You are not one of the 1%."/ Black steel in the hour of capitalism/ At 1:51 a.m.[52]*/*

51 Senate cowards/ Sold the future of the USA to lobbyists and big corporations/ For a chance to lay in bed at Trump Towers/ #TaxScamBill/ They made their bed with Trump/ Now it's every-Wealthy man-Wealthy woman-for-himself-herself-to-benefit/ Reverse-Robin Hood/

Mannn, Talk That Talk

It doesn't matter/ If you're poor White, poor Black, poor Hispanic, or poor Asian/ These Republicans really don't care about us/ This is the greatest of all "isms"/ This is about capitalism/ Economic social systems/ That values greed over humanity/ And then builds modular trailers that look like brick and mortar homes for their poor White sisters and brothers/ To convince them that they have achieved the American Dream/

Mannn, Talk That Talk

White Americans who put a criminal in the White House/ Will find before impeachment that this is not as American as Apple pie/ This is White collar crime at its finest/ White Upper-on-White Lower crime/ There is no Middle/ The rich get richer/ While the poor Whites who voted for Trump refuse to apologize to racial and ethnic minorities/ How you like them apples?!/

Mannn, Talk That Talk

November 6, 2018 and November 3, 2020/ Mark both dates on your calendar/ #VoteThemOut/ Restore the facade of American Democracy/

Eliminate American inhumanity/ And for God's sake/ Vote Trump out of office/
Hoston, 2017

THE CULTURE IS SPEAKING.

BUG IN MY EAR, PART I

An old Cat/ Once put a bug in my ear/ When it hatched/ I heard/ And I saw life differently/ He said, "Every correction is a change, but not every change is a correction."/ After he blew me that shotgun/ Contact/ He freed me from the shackles on my feet that allowed me to go there but not go there/ There is a message there/ And he answered the real question, "Who is the Nigger?"/

I hung onto every word/ His message led me to Area 51/ A place where the greater minority never have an opportunity to go/ Hidden Fences/ Black extraterrestrials/ Oppressed by the Milky Way/ Dark matter/

This conversation took on a life of its own/ Living and breathing/ And for Black male life/ That is the key to survival / Before being judged by 12, or carried by 6/ The division of life is *two* much to handle/ When we are forced to learn through trial and error/

His final words/ "Don't do good things that look bad."/ Be true to thy self/
Hoston, 2017

BUG IN MY EAR, PART II

When I was 18-years-old…

An old Cat/ On the corner/ Once showed me a wad of dreams/ Seven C-notes on top/ 20s, 10s, 5s, and 1s in the middle/ Collard green rubber band/ It was his Friday turn up/ ***Swig of liquor/***

Say young blood, "Every shuteye ain't sleep. Ya heard me. Shittttt. You better go for broke. Don't be an L7."/ Hmmmmmmmmmmm/ He was trying to tell me/ Life is not a cake walk/ Thus, I better blow out the candles/ Quick, fast, and in a hurry/ Before I age another year/ Him: "In bad things be slow, in good things be fast."/ And he showed me the C.R.E.A.M. to power his point/ Sadly, it was ineffective/

This is a '40 ounce St. Ides High Gravity Malt Liquor' in a Brown paper bag poem/ Not an 'American-style pale lager' poem/ A subconscious conversation/ Between those who know/ And those who want to understand better/ This ain't no, 'WTF is this Nigger talking about' poem/ This is a, 'I know exactly WTF this Nigga talkin' bout' poem/ This Nigga talkin' bout Black survival/

Say young blood, "A crown ain't no cure for a headache, ya heard me. Write that on your heart."/ He was preachin' the street corner gospel/ Selling words like Creflo Dollar/ But he didn't want 10%/ We just erked and jerked/ As he filled my White styrofoam cup with Brown knowledge/ A fifth of Easy Jesus/ ***Swig of liquor/*** Him: "I'm an old broom, I know these corners. Walk a straight line."/ I felt what he was saying/ Then again, it's hard to deliver the message with liquor on your breath/

Say young blood, "What you want to be when you grow up?"/ Me: "I want to run the rock."/ Him: "Nigga, I asked you what you *wanted* to be when you grow up? Stop with the bullshit."/ ***Swig of liquor/*** Him:

"Mannn, are you listening to me? Common sense is inside of your cup trying to get out. Peel off the top layer of that White styrofoam. I see now that one head cannot hold all wisdom."/ Me: "Teach me a new trick."/ **Swig of liquor**/ Him: "Life is really simple, pull the rabbit out of the hat."/

This is a 'You ain't going first in the draft' poem/ But you're still a 'Black-Brown All-American' poem/ A subconscious conversation/ Between those who know/ And those who understand that no explanation will suffice/ If you're reading this poem through White lenses/ It requires polarized lenses to reduce the glare/ To see who is speaking/ And who is listening/

Say young blood, "It's hard to stand without stepping on toes."/ **Swig of liquor**/ We sat on the egg crates/ Until the fifth could no longer bear the cross/ Him: "We all have two lives. Don't repeat either of mine."/ He then slapped me five on the Black hand side/ And said, "Whatever you become, be a good one."/
Hoston, 2017

BUG IN MY EAR, PART III

Before graduating with my Bachelor's degree and contemplating whether or not to move from New Orleans for graduate school…

An old cat/ My uncle, Robert Jr./ Once said to me on the ride to the Spur gas station in my '87 Regal/ "Neph, it's cold out here. Bundle up, lil Nigga./ You ain't shit but a caterpillar right now./ Take this cocoon of game and fly the hell outta here."/

In the store: "Give me this deuce-deuce of Milwaukee's Best and a pack of squares./ My nephew got it," he said to the clerk./ "I know you ain't think this conversation was free. When my mouth moves, my palms itch. I only scratch the left one though."/

Unc laid the game down flat/ Like an expensive cloak over a muddy puddle/ "Expose the mind, Neph./ Without battle, there is no victory./ I would hold my tongue, but silence is betrayal./ Take this G.A.M.E., ya heard me. Other than that, keep it on the playground."/
Hoston, 2017

MISSING THE MARX

The walk to the pulpit is a short one
   The doors of the church are open
   Only after burning my hand on the doorknob

"I'll walk with you."
   Said the imperfect Angel of three different names
   "No," I replied.

A fallen Angel with White gloves
   Walked me down the aisle
   To face my past

On the small wooden folding chair front-and-center of the church
   I gave my heart to the opium of the people
   And put my trust in Him

Hoston, 2017

HOW DID WE GET HERE?

There are people who I know that have gone to places but forgotten how they got there. They are now absent-minded to the world around them. Scarred by the past, these individuals were once young, vibrant, and ready to create economic, social, and political change --- revolutionary approaches for a revolutionary movement. In spite of this, the trials and tribulations of Black liberation have slowed their desires. Some are standing in memories. Others are trying to jog their memories. The rest are running straight and narrow along the path of forgotten memories. Each faction knows that Black lives have fertile meaning.

We all are frustrated by the system. Protesting for change in different ways. Each of us has to ask ourselves: Do we resist the leader of the free world -or- live in his policy-constructed world? How did we get there? What do we do? Beat ourselves up -or- allow them to knock us out?

Once tongue and cheek, they are moving forward with no clear direction. Anger is not a GPS. Frustration is not a compass. There are people moving one step at a time but marching in place --- visibility and momentum are at a standstill. Clashing ideologies about Black liberation cemented in thought.

This is a call to action. These people are us, and we are these people. We all are individuals who understand the importance of the moment. However, this is not just a moment; this is a movement. And there is no movement without all hands on deck.

We all are frustrated by the system. Protesting for change in different ways. Each of us has to ask ourselves: Do we resist the leader of the free world -or- live in his policy-constructed world? How did we get there? What do we do? Beat ourselves up -or- allow them to knock us out?
Hoston, 2017

BLACK•ISH

Four score and seven years ago/ I let my fears decide my future/ I went to a Black friend who I had once confided in/ To get Black advice/ This time/ He no longer had time to listen while eating his free lunch/ Our similar past life experiences were now viewed as different/ He changed his life's narrative/ Rewrote the Black parts/ And then forgot to let me read the Whitewashed pages/

His ego had taken him on a trip to Neverland/ An unconscious place/ Where fates are no longer linked/ A place called 'Black?ish'/ And now he refuses to return/
Hoston, 2017

I, TOO, AM FRUSTRATED

I, too, am frustrated with Black America
   the 'Cornbread and Circuses' show
   now comes with no collard greens
There are too many William O'Neal's preparing the meal
   holding the spice and seasoning
   subservient to a bland America

What happened to acknowledging all of the Black heroes?
Sheroes and heroes we will never know
They are forgotten, memories of them are bleak
Some with a gravestone, while others died alone

We culturally kill each other and are unresponsive to the heartbeat of the community. To abuse, or to be abused, that is the question. And Black folks wonder, why we 'Can't-Get-Right'? The deaths of unarmed Black men stoke anger among Black Americans, but Black men killing Black men elicit a sad calmness.

I, too, am frustrated with Black America
   we sleep Black-militant
   but we wake up White-assimilated
We leave our identity on the pillow
   and walk the earth mentally and physically misplaced
   afraid to be placed on the "agitator index"

What happened to acknowledging all of the Black heroes?
Sheroes and heroes we will never know
They are forgotten, memories of them are bleak
Some with a gravestone, while others died alone

Our only sin is our skin. But what can we do about it? They have capitalized off of the race card. We have capitalized off of the race card. It's difficult to win when no one distinguishes the Big Joker from the Little Joker, which are the two highest-ranking Trump cards in an American society that has reneged on equality.

I, too, am frustrated with Black America
   we love each other to death
   yet, we don't love each other enough
   to resuscitate each other

What happened to acknowledging all of the Black heroes?
Sheroes and heroes we will never know
They are forgotten, memories of them are bleak
Some with a gravestone, while others died alone
Hoston, 2018

IMAGINE A BLACK CULTURE…

Imagine a Black culture where all Black folks loved each other
   linked together by fate
   and consciously knowing and understanding the importance of
solidarity.

How great would it be if this truly existed?
How much love would be shared,
   among us, through us, and to dismantle hate toward us?

Some of us exist within a shell of ourselves
   not knowing but knowing, blissfully ignorant
   while others know, and do not share.
We are Indian givers to our ancestors.

Our collective identity is broken.
Do you think that what happens generally to Black people
   in this country will have something to do with what happens
   in your life? *No.*
The answer is heartbreaking.

When will the Mothership land
   gather her children
   and return them to their rightful wombs? *Next lifetime.*
The answer is painful.

Imagine a Black culture where all Black folks loved each other
   radically restructuring our human values
   and bonding together with Black love.
Hoston, 2018

MY GOD
-VS-
MY ENEMIES.

STAY WOKE.

WORK
WOKE.

ABOUT THE AUTHOR

DR. WILLIAM T. HOSTON Sr., Ph.D., is a professor, author, motivational speaker, poet, and documentarian who hails from New Orleans, Louisiana. He is associate professor of political science at the University of Houston–Clear Lake. Dr. Hoston holds research interests in the areas of minority voting behavior, political behavior of Black politicians, race and minority group behavior, Black masculinity, sexualities and gender, race and crime, and theories and dynamics of racism and oppression. His work traverses multiple genres, including editorials, essays, fiction, and poetry.

Dr. Hoston is the author or editor of fourteen books; most recently, *New Perspectives on Race and Ethnicity: Critical Readings about the Black Experience in Trump's America* (2018), *The Magic Beard* (2017), *I Love You, Son* (2017), *Race and the Black Male Subculture: The Lives of Toby Waller* (2016), *Real Niggas in Training* (2016, 2015), and *Black Masculinity in the Obama Era: Outliers of Society* (2014).

In 2013, he released the documentary, "Black Dot in a White World: Critical Discourse Among Black Males in the Obama Era," which expands the discussion of the economic, social, and political plight of black males in the Obama Era. It features the likes of Civil Rights Icon, John Lewis; Educator, Dr. Steve Perry; Urban League President, Marc Morial; Rap Icon, Master P and his son, Romeo, and a host of others that discuss what it means to be a Black male in the 21st century and the impact of living in the Obama Era (http://vimeo.com/73945114).

Dr. Hoston's motto is, "I just want to be an example. Many have come before me and hopefully those that come after will be inspired by the example that I have set."

For more information on Dr. Hoston, please visit:
http://www.WilliamHoston.com

LIST OF PREVIOUS AND FORTHCOMING BOOKS

Race Relations, Race and Crime, Black Masculinity, and Black LGBTQIA
Black Masculinity in the Obama Era: Outliers of Society (2014)

Race and the Black Male Subculture: The Lives of Toby Waller (2016)

New Perspectives on Race and Ethnicity: Critical Readings about the Black Experience in Trump's America (2018)

Toxic Silence: Race, Black Gender Identity, and Addressing the Violence against Black Transgender Women in Houston, TX (Forthcoming, 2018)

Children's Books
No Bullies in the Huddle –Philadelphia Eagles, Washington Redskins (2013, 2015)

Dr. William Jr. Presents: The Magic Beard (2017)

Poetry Books
Real Niggas in Training (2015, 2016)

I Love You, Son: Words to His Soul (2017)

Power to the People: Ascending Beyond Racism (2018)

Motivational Success Books
Listen to Me Now, Or Listen to Me Later: A Memoir of Academic Success for College Students, Ed. I (2012)

Listen to Me Now, Or Listen to Me Later: A Memoir of Academic Success for College Students, Ed. II (2014)

Listen to Me Now, Or Listen to Me Later: A Memoir of Academic Success for College Students, Ed. III (Forthcoming, 2018)

Why "We" Didn't Choose You - Relationship Series Books
WWDCY, Vol. I: A Relationship Handbook for Women (and Men) (2010)

WWDCY, Vol. II: Poetic Love: The Joy of Happiness (2014)

WWDCY, Vol. III: From a Woman's Perspective (2016)

WWDCY, Vol. I: A Relationship Handbook for Women (and Men) – Reloaded (2016)

NOT EVERY ONE HAS UNTIL MONDAY
(Jacob Lara, 1996 - 2016)[53]

No one looks forward to Mondays
   But for Jacob, it was to be a redirection of his life
   A life that ended in the blink of an eye

Jacob died on Friday morning
   On Thursday morning, we worked out together at the gym
   He promised to meet me on Monday
   To enroll in college

During our workout
   We talked about life, his new girlfriend, wanting more tattoos,
   And him wanting to buy a gun

We all know that *facts are stubborn things*[54]
   Especially to young people
   Therefore, I spared him the talk and said, "Be careful."
Jacob replied, "I know, big dawg. I got you."

It went over his head
   And came back to me like a boomerang
   I never thought the recoil would happen so soon

On Friday morning, around 12:20 a.m.
   His girlfriend accidentally shot him
   She called 911, but it was too late

This accident posed a teachable moment
   Unfortunately, I never got the chance to formally teach Jacob

I love you, Jacob. Rest in Paradise.
Hoston, 2018

Endnotes

[1] According to the *2018 Presidents & Executive Politics Presidential Greatness Survey* conducted from December 22, 2017 to January 16, 2018, President Donald J. Trump ranked as the worst president ever (12.34 average rating). The survey created a ranking of presidential greatness that covered all presidents from George Washington to Donald Trump. Barack H. Obama ranked at 8th (71.13 average rating). Available at: https://sps.boisestate.edu/politicalscience/files/2018/02/Greatness.pdf.

[2] Euripides.

[3] On September 18, 1858, during a campaign speech while running against Stephen A. Douglas of Illinois for a U.S. Senate seat, Lincoln said:

> I will say then that I am not, nor ever have been in favor of bringing about in anyway the social and political equality of the White and Black races – that I am not nor ever have been in favor of making voters or jurors of Negroes, nor of qualifying them to hold office, nor to intermarry with White people; and I will say in addition to this that there is a physical difference between the White and Black races which I believe will forever forbid the two races living together on terms of social and political equality. And inasmuch as they cannot so live, while they do remain together there must be the position of superior and inferior, and I as much as any other man am in favor of having the superior position assigned to the White race.

[4] Maze featuring Frankie Beverly, "I Wanna Thank You" in *We Are One*. (CD; Capitol Records, 1983). Available at: https://www.youtube.com/watch?v=s_tSafngm-E.

[5] See Hot 97 (2017, December 14). *Black Thought freestyles on Flex | #Freestyle087* [Video file]. Retrieved from: https://www.youtube.com/watch?v=prmQgSpV3fA.

[6] Transcript of the original speech available at: https://www.

archives.gov/files/press/exhibits/dream-speech.pdf.

[7] Akiro Kurosawa.

[8] Transcript of the Thomas Jefferson speech available at: http://www.history.org/almanack/life/politics/sumview.cfm.

[9] The Dramatics, "Hey You! Get Off My Mountain" in *The Dramatic Experience*. (CD; Volt Records, 1973). Available at: https://www.youtube.com/watch?v=ymVAVVJQ2KM.

[10] "Free, White, and 21" is a catchphrase to define White privilege. See Heisel, A. 2015. "The rise and fall of an All-American catchphrase: 'Free, White, and 21.'" *Pictorial.jezebel.com*. Available at: https://pictorial.jezebel.com/the-rise-and-fall-of-an-all-american-catchphrase-free-1729621311 (September 10).

[11] Cartwright, S. A. "Report on the diseases and physical peculiarities of the Negro race," in *The New Orleans Medical and Surgical Journal* (May 1851) 7:691-715.

[12] Stowe, H. B. *Uncle Tom's cabin*. Dover thrift ed. New York: Dover Publications, 2005.

[13] Sam Cooke, "Mean Old World" in *Night Beat*. (Album; RCA Records, 1963). Available at: https://www.youtube.com/watch?v=GubqKReuIsw.

[14] Ray Charles, "Hard Times" in *The Genius Sings the Blues*. (Album; Atlantic Records, 1961). Available at: https://www.youtube.com/watch?v=_9T-RA6lk9U.

[15] See Spuddy83 (2010, August 7). *Gil Scott-Heron - The Revolution Will Not Be Televised* [Video file]. Retrieved from: https://www.youtube.com/watch?v=qGaoXAwl9kw.

[16] Portions of this piece were previously published. Rights and permissions for the following excerpt were obtained from Kendall Hunt Publishing Company.

[17] In total it was 90 executive orders including presidential memoranda (28) and proclamations (30). A full list of executive orders, available at: https://www.whitehouse.gov/briefing-room/presidential-actions/executive-orders.

[18] See Langer, G. 2017. "President Trump at 100 days: No honeymoon but no regrets (POLL)." *ABCNews.com*. Available at: http://

abcnews.go.com/Politics/president-trump-100-days-honeymoon-regrets-poll/story?id=46943338 (April 23).

[19] *Ibid*, President Trump at 100 days

[20] *Ibid*, President Trump at 100 days

[21] See Lima, C. 2017. "Trump: I thought presidency would be 'easier' than 'previous life.'" *Politico.com*. Available at: http://www.politico.com/story/2017/04/28/trump-presidency-easier-previous-life-237728 (April 28).

[22] See Parham, J. 2015. "The collected quotes of Donald Trump on "the Blacks."" *Gawker.com*. Available at: http://gawker.com/the-collected-quotes-of-donald-trump-on-the-blacks-1719961925 (July 24).

[23] In the 2016 presidential election, eight percent of Black Americans voted for Trump.

[24] See LoBianco, T., and A. Killough. 2016. "Trump pitches black voters: 'What the hell do you have to lose?'" *CNN.com*. Available at:http://www.cnn.com/2016/08/19/politics/donald-trump-african-american-voters (August 19).

[25] See Johnson, J. 2016. "Donald Trump to African American and Hispanic voters: 'What do you have to lose?'" *WashingtonPost.com*. Available at: https://www.washingtonpost.com/news/post-politics/wp/2016/08/22/donald-trump-to-african-american-and-hispanic-voters-what-do-you-have-to-lose/?utm_term=.e07dae94504e (August 22).

[26] See Urbanski, D. 2016. "'This was a white-lash against a black president': Angry Van Jones decries Trump election." *TheBlaze.com*. Available at: http://www.theblaze.com/news/2016/11/09/this-was-a-white-lash-against-a-black-president-angry-van-jones-decries-trump-election (November 9).

[27] See @ DrDavidDuke (2017, January 20). Retrieved from: https://twitter.com/drdavidduke/status/822489438479650816.

[28] According to August 2017 data from the Southern Poverty Law Center, there are 917 hate-groups currently operating in the USA. Data available at: https://www.splcenter.org/hate-map.

[29] See Scott, E. 2016. "Donald Trump: I'm 'the least racist person.'" *CNN.com*. Available at: http://www.cnn.com/2016/09/15/politics/donald-trump-election-2016-racism (September 15).

³⁰ See Pyke, A. 2017. "'Trump is setting us free:' White supremacists celebrate reports that Trump will dial down scrutiny." *ThinkProgress.org*. Available at: https://thinkprogress.org/trump-is-setting-us-free-white-supremacists-celebrate-reports-that-trump-will-dial-down-scrutiny-136039e12fad (February 3).

³¹ See the details of the message, "Standing up for our law enforcement community." Available at: https://www.whitehouse.gov/law-enforcement-community.

³² See Lavender, P. 2017. "44 leaders, legislators and artists sum up Trump's first 100 days." *HuffingtonPost.com*. Available at: http://www.huffingtonpost.com/entry/donald-trump-100-days-quotes_us_58fe5594e4b00fa7de16c10c?ncid=tweetlnkushpmg00000051&section=us_black-voices (April 29).

³³ *Ibid*, Donald Trump to African American and Hispanic voters: 'What do you have to lose?

³⁴ According to 2013 data from the National Center for Education Statistics, just 6 percent of full-time faculty members were Black and 5 percent were Latino.

³⁵ Bronstein et al. (1993), in their study of barriers to academic careers for women and ethnic minorities, indicates that tenure committees often view race and gender-specific publication outlets as inferior. Those who publish in them are incapable of landing their research in "prestigious" and "traditional" academic journals. See Bronstein, P., Rothblum, E. D., and S. E. Solomon. 1993. Ivy halls and glass walls: Barriers to academic careers for women and ethnic minorities. In R. Boice and J. Gainen (Eds.), *New directions for teaching and learning* (17-31). San Francisco: Jossey-Bass.

³⁶ Ladson-Billings, G. "Silences as weapons: Challenges of a Black professor teaching White students," in *Situated Pedagogies: Classroom Practices in Postmodern Times* (Spring, 1996) 35(2):79-85.

³⁷ Roots. Directed by David L. Wolper Productions. American Broadcasting Company, 1977.

³⁸ Saint Teresa Benedicta of the Cross; Edith Stein.

³⁹ Definitions: (1) SJWs = Social justice warrior; (2) Muh oppression = The notion that preferential treatment is provided to women

and racial and ethnic minorities; and (3) "14/88" = A combination of two popular White supremacist numeric symbols. First, 14 words slogan: "We must secure the existence of our people and a future for white children." Second, 88, which stands for "Heil Hitler" (H being the 8th letter of the alphabet). More information is available at: https://www.adl.org/education/references/hate-symbols/1488.

[40] See the *Know Your Rights Camp* website. Available at: http://knowyourrightscamp.com/about.

[41] Rhoden, W. C. *Forty million dollar slaves: The rise, fall, and redemption of the black athlete.* New York, NY: Broadway Books, 2007.

[42] Diamond Reynolds' 4-year-old daughter after St. Anthony police officer, Jeronimo Yanez, fired seven times at Philando Castile.

[43] Portions of this piece were previously published. Rights and permissions for the following excerpt were obtained from Palgrave Macmillan and Springer Nature.

[44] For more information on the game, "Hit the Nigger Baby," see the 1996 *Dictionary of American Regional English, Volume III, I-O*.Available at: http://projects.iq.harvard.edu/files/cb45/files/20101119151543252.pdf.

[45] See Hastings, D. 2015. "South Dakota gun show seller defends using racist posters for target practice." *DailyNews.com*. Available at: http://www.nydailynews.com/news/national/s-gun-show-vendor-booted-racist-target-sheets-article-1.2152926 (March 17).

[46] See Izadi, E. 2015. "Florida police used mugshots of black men for target practice. Clergy responded: #UseMeInstead." *WashingtonPost.com*. Available at:http://www.washingtonpost.com/news/morning-mix/wp/2015/01/25/florida-police-used-mugshots-of-black-men-for-target-practice-clergy-responded-usemeinstead (January 25).

[47] See Barbash, F. 2015. "Florida police department caught using African American mug shots for target practice." *WashingtonPost.com*. Available at: http://www.washingtonpost.com/news/morning-mix/wp/2015/01/16/florida-police-department-caught-using-african-american-mug-shots-for-target-practice (January 16).

[48] *Ibid*, Florida police department caught using African American mug shots for target practice

[49] *Ibid*, Florida police department caught using African American mug shots for target practice

[50] See *CNN News* article, "Woman sees images of black males as sniper targets; one is her brother." Available at: http://www.cnn.com/2015/01/16/us/florida-black-male-sniper-targets (January 19, 2015).

[51] See Coates, T. 2017. "My president was black." *TheAtlantic.com*. Available at: https://www.theatlantic.com/magazine/archive/2017/01/my-president-was-black/508793 (January/February).

[52] Public Enemy, "Black Steel in the Hour of Chaos" in *It Takes a Nation of Millions to Hold Us Back*. (CD; Def Jam Records, 1989). Available at: https://www.youtube.com/watch?v=ZM5_6js19eM.

[53] From his obituary: "Jacob was an outgoing, loving young man that enjoyed sports cars, cheering on his favorite sports teams and working out. He had a huge infectious smile even if sometimes it was mischievous and always felt it was important to look good for the ladies. Jacob will be greatly missed by all that knew and loved him." Available at: http://claytonfuneralhomes.com/tribute/details/1369/Jacob-Lara/obituary.html.

[54] John Adams.

www.ingramcontent.com/pod-product-compliance
Lightning Source LLC
Chambersburg PA
CBHW061330040426
42444CB00011B/2853